AN
AMERICAN
SUNRISE

Conflict Resolutions for Holy Beings

Crazy Brave: A Memoir

Soul Talk, Song Language: Conversations with Joy Harjo

For a Girl Becoming

She Had Some Horses

How We Became Human: New and Selected Poems

A Map to the Next World

The Good Luck Cat

Reinventing the Enemy's Language:
Contemporary Native Women's Writing of North America

The Spiral of Memory

The Woman Who Fell from the Sky

Fishing

In Mad Love and War

Secrets from the Center of the World

What Moon Drove Me to This?

The Last Song

MUSIC ALBUMS

Red Dreams, A Trail Beyond Tears

Winding Through the Milky Way

She Had Some Horses

Native Joy for Real

Letter from the End of the Twentieth Century

PLAYS

We Were There When Jazz Was Invented

Wings of Night Sky, Wings of Morning Light

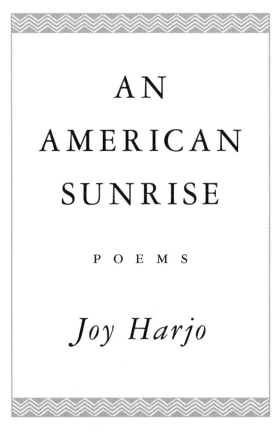

AN AMERICAN SUNRISE

POEMS

Joy Harjo

W. W. NORTON & COMPANY
Independent Publishers Since 1923

For information about permission to reproduce selections from this book,
write to Permissions, W. W. Norton & Company, Inc.,
500 Fifth Avenue, New York, NY 10110

For information about special discounts for bulk purchases, please contact
W. W. Norton Special Sales at specialsales@wwnorton.com or 800-233-4830

Manufacturing by Versa Press
Book design by JAM Design
Production manager: Beth Steidle

Library of Congress Cataloging-in-Publication Data

Names: Harjo, Joy, author.
Title: An American sunrise : poems / Joy Harjo.
Description: First edition. | New York : W. W. Norton & Company, 2019.
Identifiers: LCCN 2019021562 | ISBN 9781324003861 (hardcover)
Classification: LCC PS3558.A62423 A64 2019 | DDC 811/.54—dc23
LC record available at https://lccn.loc.gov/2019021562

W. W. Norton & Company, Inc., 500 Fifth Avenue, New York, N.Y. 10110
www.wwnorton.com

W. W. Norton & Company Ltd., 15 Carlisle Street, London W1D 3BS

2 3 4 5 6 7 8 9 0

For the children, so they may find their way through the dark—

They are all our children.

To heal was to be familiar with what destroyed.

　—RAY YOUNG BEAR, Meskwaki poet

After our walk, there were no babies left;
they killed the babies.

　—JAMES SCOTT, Mvskoke elder and survivor
　　of the Trail of Tears

When you act and speak you must think of all your
relatives—known and unknown. You must also
remember the plants, the animals, the living things,
and the ancient ones—those that have gone before you.

　—HIYVTKE (JEAN CHAUDHURI), Mvskoke,
　　2001

To tell the truth is to become beautiful, to begin to love
yourself, value yourself. And that's political, in its most
profound way.

　—JUNE JORDAN, Caribbean-American poet

CONTENTS

Prologue   x v
Map of the Trail of Tears   x v i i

Break My Heart   3

My grandfather Monahwee   5

Exile of Memory   6

Granddaughters   2 0

The Fight   2 1

Directions to You   2 2

Seven Generations   2 5

In 1990 a congress   2 6

Weapons,   2 7

The Story Wheel   2 8

Once I looked at the moon   2 9

Washing My Mother's Body   3 0

There is a map   3 4

Rising and Falling   3 5

The Road to Disappearance   3 6

Mama and Papa Have the Going Home Shiprock Blues   3 7

My great-grandfather Monahwee   4 6

How to Write a Poem in a Time of War   4 7

Mvskoke Mourning Song   5 1

First Morning   5 2

Singing Everything   5 3

Falling from the Night Sky   54

Our knowledge is based   55

For Earth's Grandsons   56

Running   57

A Refuge in the Smallest of Places   59

I'm Nobody! Who Are You?   60

Bourbon and Blues   61

My Great-Aunt Ella Monahwee Jacobs's Testimony   63

Road   64

The Southeast was covered   65

Desire's Dog   66

Dawning   67

Honoring   68

My Man's Feet   70

"I Wonder What You Are Thinking,"   72

For Those Who Would Govern   74

Rabbit Invents the Saxophone   75

When Adolfe Sax patented   77

Let There Be No Regrets   78

Advice for Countries, Advanced, Developing and Falling   79

Tobacco Origin Story   81

My aunt Lois Harjo told me   83

Redbird Love   84

We follow the DNA spiral of stories   86

Becoming Seventy   87

Beyond   95

Ren-Toh-Pvrv   96

Memory Sack   97

Every night   98

Cehotosakvtes   99

One March   100

By the Way   101

When we made it down last year   103

Welcoming Song   104

An American Sunrise   105

Bless This Land   106

Acknowledgments   111

On May 28, 1830, President Andrew Jackson unlawfully signed the Indian Removal Act to force move southeastern peoples from our homelands to the West. We were rounded up with what we could carry. We were forced to leave behind houses, printing presses, stores, cattle, schools, pianos, ceremonial grounds, tribal towns, churches. We witnessed immigrants walking into our homes with their guns, Bibles, household goods and families, taking what had been ours, as we were surrounded by soldiers and driven away like livestock at gunpoint.

There were many trails of tears of tribal nations all over North America of indigenous peoples who were forcibly removed from their homelands by government forces.

The indigenous peoples who are making their way up from the southern hemisphere are a continuation of the Trail of Tears.

May we all find the way home.

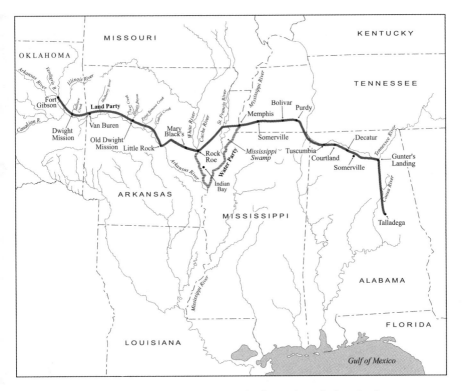

MISSOURI

KENTUCKY

OKLAHOMA

TENNESSEE

Arkansas River

Verdigris R.

Illinois River

Mulberry River

Fort
Gibson

Clear Creek

Cadron Creek
Piney Bottom Creek
Point Remove Creek

Canadian R.

Land Party

Mississippi River

Bolivar   Purdy

Dwight
Mission

Van Buren

Mary
Black's

Cache River

White River

St. Francis River

Memphis

Old Dwight
Mission   Little Rock

Rock
Roe

Water Party

Mississippi
Swamp

Somerville

Tuscumbia

Decatur

Courtland

Somerville

Gunter's
Landing

Tennessee River

Arkansas River

ARKANSAS

Indian
Bay

MISSISSIPPI

Talladega

Coosa River

Mississippi River

ALABAMA

FLORIDA

LOUISIANA

Gulf of Mexico

*This is only one trail. There were many trails of tears from the homelands
of the Muscogee Creek Nation west, just as there were for the Cherokee,
Chickasaw, Choctaw, Seminole and many other tribal nations.*

AN
AMERICAN
SUNRISE

BREAK MY HEART

There are always flowers,
Love cries, or blood.

Someone is always leaving
By exile, death, or heartbreak.

The heart is a fist.
It pockets prayer or holds rage.

It's a timekeeper.
Music maker, or backstreet truth teller.

Baby, baby, baby
You can't say what's been said

Before, though even words
Are creatures of habit.

You cannot force poetry
With a ruler, or jail it at a desk.

Mystery is blind, but wills you
To untie the cloth, in eternity.

Police with their guns
Cannot enter here to move us off our lands.

History will always find you, and wrap you
In its thousand arms.

. . .

Someone will lift from the earth
Without wings.

Another will fall from the sky
Through the knots of a tree.

Chaos is primordial.
All words have roots here.

You will never sleep again
Though you will never stop dreaming.

The end can only follow the beginning.
And it will zigzag through time, governments, and lovers.

Be who you are, even if it kills you.

It will. Over and over again.
Even as you live.

Break my heart, why don't you?

My grandfather Monahwee (also spelled "Menawa"), of some generations back, was allowed to visit his home, at Okfuskee (near what is now known as Dadeville, Alabama), to stay there one night before being exiled to the West. He is reported to have said to "a highly reputable gentleman," after gifting him with his portrait:

"I am going away. I have brought you this picture—I wish you to take it and hang it up in your house, that when your children look at it, you can tell them what I have been . . . for when I cross the great river, my desire is that I may never again see the face of a white man."

After he left, he never turned back. He kept walking forward with his beloved people.

I returned to see what I would find, in these lands we were forced to leave behind.

EXILE OF MEMORY

Do not return,
We were warned by one who knows things
You will only upset the dead.
They will emerge from the spiral of little houses
Lined up in the furrows of marrow
And walk the land.
There will be no place in memory
For what they see
The highways, the houses, the stores of interlopers
Perched over the blood fields
Where the dead last stood.
And then what, you with your words
In the enemy's language,
Do you know how to make a peaceful road
Through human memory?
And what of angry ghosts of history?
Then what?

. . .

Don't look back.

In Sunday school we were told Lot's wife
Looked back and turned
To salt.
But her family wasn't leaving Paradise.
We loved our trees and waters
And the creatures and earths and skies
In that beloved place.
Those beings were our companions
Even as they fed us, cared for us.
If I turn to salt
It will be of petrified tears
From the footsteps of my relatives
As they walked west.

. . .

I did not know what I would find

The first night we set up our bed in the empty room
Of our condo above the Tennessee River
They'd heard we were coming
Those who continued to keep the land
Despite the imposition of newcomers
And the forced exile of our relatives.

All night, they welcomed us
All night, the stomp dancers
All night, the shell shakers
All night circle after circle made a spiral
To the Milky Way

.   .   .

We are still in mourning.

The children were stolen from these beloved lands by the government.
Their hair was cut, their toys and handmade clothes ripped
From them. They were bathed in pesticides
And now clean, given prayers in a foreign language to recite
As they were lined up to sleep alone in their army-issued cages.

. . .

Grief is killing us. Anger tormenting us. Sadness eating us with disease.
Our young women are stolen, raped and murdered.
Our young men are killed by the police, or killing themselves and
   each other.

. . .

This is a warning:
Heroin is a fool companion offering freedom from the gauntlet of history.
Meth speeds you past it.
Alcohol, elixir of false bravado, will take you over the edge of it.
Enough chemicals and processed craving
And you can't push away from the table.

If we pay enough, maybe we can buy ourselves back.

. . .

We used to crowd the bar for Tuesday ten-cent beer night.
It was the Indian, poetry, biker and student bar
In that university and military base town.
Trays packed with small cups of beer passed nonstop
Over the counter all night.
We brought all of our thirsty dreams there
Gambled with them at the pool table, all night.
Danced with them and each other on the blood-stained dance floor
To jukebox songs fed by dimes and quarters, all night.
And by 2 A.M. we staggered out
To the world made by Puritan dreaming
No place for Indians, poets or any others who would
Ride the wild winds for dangerous knowledge.

All night.

.　　.　　.

In the complex here there is a singing tree.
It sings of the history of the trees here.
It sings of Monahwee who stood with his warrior friends
On the overlook staring into the new town erected
By illegal residents.
It sings of the Civil War camp, the bloodied
The self-righteous, and the forsaken.
It sings of atomic power and the rise
Of banks whose spires mark
The worship places.
The final verse is always the trees.
They will remain.

. . .

When it is time to leave this place of return,
What will I say that I found here?

From out of the mist, a form wrestled to come forth—
It was many-legged, of many arms, and sent forth thoughts of
    many colors.
There were deer standing near us under the parted, misted sky
As we watched, they smelled for water
Green light entered their bodies
From all leaved things they ate—

. . .

The old Mvskoke laws outlawed the Christian religion
Because it divided the people.
We who are relatives of Panther, Raccoon, Deer, and the other
    animals and winds were soon divided.
But Mvskoke ways are to make relatives.
We made a relative of Jesus, gave him a Mvskoke name.

. . .

We could not see our ancestors as we climbed up
To the edge of destruction
But from the dark we felt their soft presences at the edge of our
    mind
And we heard their singing.

There is no word in this trade language, no words with enough
    power to hold all this we have become—

. . .

We are in time. There is no time, in time.
We are in a traditional Mvskoke village, far back in time.
Ekvnvjakv is in labor, so long in time.
She is not young and beyond the time of giving birth.
The keeper of birthing is tracking her energy, and time.
My thinking is questioning how, this time.

. . .

A young boy wrestles with two puppies at the doorway.
A little girl, bearing an old woman spirit appears
With green plants in her hands.
Twins play around the edge of the bed.

Earth's womb tightens with the need to push.
That is all that I see because of the fogginess of time.

. . .

I sing my leaving song.
I sing it to the guardian trees, this beloved earth,
To those who stay here to care for memory.
I will sing it until the day I die.

GRANDDAUGHTERS

I was a thought, a dream, a fish, a wing
And then a human being
When I emerged from my mother's river
On my father's boat of potent fever
I carried a sack of dreams from a starlit dwelling
To be opened when I begin bleeding
There's a red dress, deerskin moccasins
The taste of berries made of promises
While the memories shift in their skins
At every moon, to do their ripening

THE FIGHT

The rising sun paints the feet
Of night-crawling enemies.
And they scatter into the burning hills.
I have fought each of them.
I know them by name.
From before I could speak.
I've used every weapon.
To make them retreat.
Yet they return every night
If I don't keep guard
They elbow through openings in faith
Tear the premise of trust
And stick their shields through the doubt of smoke
To challenge me.
I grow tired of the heartache
Of every small and large war
Passed from generation
To generation.
But it is not in me to give up.
I was taught to give honor to the house of the warriors
Which cannot exist without the house of the peacemakers.

DIRECTIONS TO YOU
Rainy Dawn Ortiz

Follow them, stop, turn around
Go the other way.
Left, right,
Mine, yours.
We become lost,
Unsteady.
Take a deep breath,
Pray.
You will not always be lost.
You are right here,
In your time,
In your place.

1. North
Star, guidance as we look up
To the brightest white
Hoping it leads you to where you want to go,
Hoping that it knows where you should be.
We find our peace here in the white,
Gather our strength, our breath, and learn how to be.

2. East
The sun rises,
Red,
Morning heat on our face even on the coldest morning.
The sun creates life,
Energy,
Nourishment.
Gather strength, pull it in
Be right where you are.

3. South
Butterfly flits
Spreads yellow beauty.
We have come to this moment in time
Step by step,
We don't always listen to directions,
We let the current carry us,
Push us,
Force us along the path.
We stumble,
Get up and keep moving.

4. West
Sunsets, brings
Darkness,
Brings black.
We find solitude,
Time to take in breath and
Pray.
Even in darkness you
Can be found.
Call out even in a whisper
Or whimper,
You will be heard.

To find,
To be found,
To be understood,
To be seen,
Heard, felt.
You are,
Breath.
You are,
Memory.

You are,
Touch.
You are,
Right here.

SEVEN GENERATIONS

Children play with full bellies
At the edge of the mating dance.
Beneath a sky thrown open
To the need of stars
To know themselves against the dark.
All night we dance the weave of joy and tears
All night we're lit with the sunrise of forever
Just ahead of us, through the trees
One generation after the other.

In 1990 a congress of indigenous peoples met outside of Quito, Ecuador, to discuss the Columbian Quincentenary, a celebration by immigrant populations of the arrival of Christopher Columbus to the western hemisphere on his financed expedition to find a trade route to India. Tribal people came from all of the Americas and met to discuss the destructive and monumental changes since this European explorer's arrival. We met together to gain insight and strength and ponder how we would continue to move forward past the massive destruction and disrespect of the earth mind, body and spirit, and to continue our sovereignty as Native nations.

In the women's circle, a striking Bolivian Indian woman in a bowler hat stood up. She welcomed us, and noted that she was surprised at all of the Natives attending from the United States.

"We thought John Wayne had killed all of you."

(This was not a joke.)

"And why," she asked, "Do you call yourselves America? This hemisphere is one body, one person. *She* is America."

WEAPONS,

OR WHAT I HAVE TAKEN IN MY HAND TO SPEAK WHEN I HAVE NO WORDS
(inspired by T. C. Cannon's images)

BLACK—Before there was anything else possible. We settled there, not far from the river, at the ragged edge of night. There were no words for eyes or light, or even being. Imagination took its first breath, while we were camped there in the nowhere.

YELLOW—We struck up a conversation. Somebody opened their hands with food. The drum brought forth the language of the earth. An elder woman's voice urged the stars out of their houses to come dance with us. A young man followed with a new song that brought excitement to the young women wrapped in shawls who were dancing, and brought forth ancestors who danced with us.

RED—Each of us is a wave in the river of humanity. If we break we bleed out. If we move forward together we are bound together by scarlet waters of belief. One side is war. One side feeds the generations. We are bright with the need for life.

GREEN—After winter snow, after you have left, after giving up, after the planting, after letting the horses free to roam, after the loving, after yes, never no. The grasses rise up from the earth to answer the winds in song. After I rise up with this shimmering love to sing.

BLUE—If you really love me sweetheart you would not forsake me here at the dawn of forever. I will always love you, always, sang the sky to eternity. I will meet you there, at the seamless edge of sunrise.

THE STORY WHEEL

I leave you to your ceremony of grieving
Which is also of celebration
Given when an honored humble one
Leaves behind a trail of happiness
In the dark of human tribulation.
None of us is above the other
In this story of forever.
Though we follow that red road home,
one behind another.
There is a light breaking through the storm
And it is buffalo hunting weather.
There you can see your mother.
She is busy as she was ever—
She holds up a new jingle dress, for her youngest beloved daughter.
And for her special son, a set of finely beaded gear.
All for that welcome home dance,
The most favorite of all—
when everyone finds their way back together
to dance, eat and celebrate.
And tell story after story
of how they fought and played
in the story wheel
and how no one
was ever really lost at all.

Once I looked at the moon and caught sight of a strange thing.
A cricket had perched upon the handrail, only a few inches away
from me. My line of vision was such that the creature filled the
moon like a fossil. It had gone there, I thought, to live and die, for
there, of all places, was its small definition made whole and eternal.
A warm wind rose up and purled like the longing within me.

—N. Scott Momaday, *The Way to Rainy Mountain,* 1969

Until the passage of the Indian Religious Freedom Act of 1978,
it was illegal for Native citizens to practice our cultures. This
included the making and sharing of songs and stories. Songs and
stories in one culture are poetry and prose in another. They are
intrinsic to cultural sovereignty. To write or create as a Native
person was essentially illegal.

WASHING MY MOTHER'S BODY

I never got to wash my mother's body when she died.
I return to take care of her in memory.
That's how I make peace when things are left undone.
I go back and open the door.
I step in to make my ritual. To do what should have been done,
what needs to be fixed so that my spirit can move on,
So that the children and grandchildren are not caught in a knot
Of regret they do not understand.

I find the white enamel pan she used for bread and biscuits.
It is the same pan she used to bathe us when we were babies.
I turn the faucet on and hold my hand under the water
until it is warm, the temperature one uses to wash an infant.
I find a clean washcloth in a stack of washcloths.
She had nothing in her childhood.
She made sure she had plenty of everything
when she grew up and made her own life.
Her closets were full of pretty dresses,
so many she had not time to wear them all.
They were bought by the young girl who wore the same
    flour sack dress
to school every day, the one she had to wash out every night,
and hang up to dry near the wood stove.

I pick up the bar of soap from her sink,
the same soap she used yesterday morning to wash her face.
When she looked in the mirror, did she know it would be her
    last sunrise?
I move over pill bottles, a clock radio on the table by the bed,
a pen, and set down the pan. I straighten the blankets over her,

to keep her warm, for dignity.
I start with her face. Her face is unlined even two months before
her eightieth birthday. She was known for her beauty,
and when younger passed for the Cherokee
that she was through her mother and her mother's mother
all the way back to time's beginning.
My mother had the iron pot given to her by her Cherokee mother,
whose mother gave it to her, given to her by the U.S. government
on the Trail of Tears.
She grew flowers in it.

As I wash my mother's face, I tell her
how beautiful she is, how brave, how her beauty and bravery
live on in her grandchildren. Her face is relaxed, peaceful.
Her earth memory body has not left yet,
but when I see her the next day, embalmed and in the casket
in the funeral home, it will be gone.
Where does it go?
It is heavier than the spirit who lifted up and flew.
I think of it making the rounds to every place it has loved to say
    goodbye.
Goodbye to the house where I brought my babies home, she sings.
Goodbye to June's Bar where I was the shuffleboard queen.

I cannot say goodbye yet.
I will never say goodbye.

I lift up each arm to wash. Her hands still wear her favorite rings.
She loved her body and decorated it with shiny jewelry,
with creams and makeup.
I am tender over that burn scar on her arm,
From when she cooked at the place with the cruel boss
who insisted she reach her hand into the Fryolator to clean it.

She had protested it was still hot, and suffered a deep burn.
That scar always reminded me of her coming in
from working long hours in restaurants,
her uniform drenched with sweat, determination and exhaustion.
Once she came home and I was burning up with a fever.
She pulled out the same pan I am dipping the washcloth in now,
only she's added rubbing alcohol, to bring the fever down.
She washes tenderly, tells me about how her friend Chunkie
left her husband again, how she knows her old boss,
a Jewish woman who treated her kindly,
has cancer. She doesn't know how she knows;
she just knows.
She doesn't tell me that—
I find it in a journal she has left me,
a day book in which she has written notes
for me to find when she is gone.

I wash her neck and lift the blankets to move down her heart.
I thank her body for carrying us through the tough story.
through the violence of my father, and her second husband.
Her mother's mother died when she was born
and her adoptive mother, another Cherokee woman,
had no love in her heart for a tiny girl
whose light hair betrayed her Indian-ness,
unlike the baby's older, darker sister who would stay
within their circle.
Because her mother was not there for her,
My grandmother did not know how to mother my mother.

The story is all there, in her body, as I wash her to prepare her
to be let down into earth, and return all stories to the earth.
My body memories rise up as I wash.
I recall carrying my two children, rocking them,

and feeding them from my body.
How I knew myself as beloved Earth, in that body.

I uncover my mother's legs.
I remember the varicose veins that swelled like rivers
when my mother would get off a long shift of standing and
     cooking.
They carried more than a woman should carry.
A woman should be honored like a queen,
traditionally we treated our women with that kind of respect,
my Creek husband tells me.
Ha, I laugh and ask him, "then why aren't you cooking my
     dinner?"
I wash her feet, caress them.
You will have some rest now, I tell my mother,
even as I know my mother was never one for resting.
I cover her.

I make the final wring of the washcloth and drape it over the pan.
I brush my mother's hair and kiss her forehead.
I ask the keepers of the journey to make sure her travel is safe
     and sure.
I ask the angels, whom she loved and with whom she spoke
     frequently,
to take her home, but wait, not before I find her favorite perfume.
Then I sing her favorite song, softly.
I don't know the name of the song, just a few phrases,
one of those old homemade heartbreak songs
where there's a moment of happiness
wound through—

and then I let her go.

There is a map, a series of maps that are t/here and have always been t/here. They are transparent and layered, one on top of another. One generation over another, the lines of connection are relentlessly weaving, patterning rhythmically, mythically, and historically by image, sound and sense. Each map is a being with a mouth and a tail, even as it is a field of ocean or grass. They are making helixes of memory; memory is always moving.

My mother was a songwriter and singer. She is William Blake's "Little lamb, who made thee / Dost thou know who made thee?" and Alfred Lord Tennyson. She is the traditional Cherokee songs sung at her aunt's funeral. She is the "Burning Ring of Fire" running away to Independence, Kansas, at sixteen. She is "Crazy" sung by Patsy Cline in a wake of heartache. That was my mother, singing, all those years. My mother's gifts were trampled by economic necessity and emotional imprisonment.

My father was a dancer, a rhythm keeper. His ancestors were orators, painters, tribal chiefs, stomp dancers, preachers, and speakers. His mother was a saxophone player and painter in Indian Territory before Oklahoma statehood. All his relatively short life he looked for a vision or song to counter the heartache of history.

Rivers are the old roads, as are songs, to traverse memory.

I emerged from the story, dripping with the waters of memory.

RISING AND FALLING

Human poetry is a restless soul
And does not always know what it holds,
When it is regaling beloved guests at a table
Graced with food and drink. What
Songs of tempestuous rising and falling,
One country after another.

THE ROAD TO DISAPPEARANCE

"The Indians will vanish" has been the talk of the older Indians ever since the white people first came to mingle among them. They seemed to prophesy that the coming of the white man would not be for their good and when the step toward their removal to a country to the west was just beginning, it was the older Indians who remarked and talked about themselves by saying, "Now, the Indian is now on the road to disappearance." This had reference to their leaving of their ways, their familiar surroundings where their customs were performed, their medicine, their hunting grounds and their friends.

When they had reached their new homes in the Indian Territory, their conversations were about their old homes and they said, "We have started on the road that leads to our disappearance and we are facing the evening of our existence and are nearly at the end of the trail that we trod when we were forced to leave our homes in Alabama and Georgia. In time, perhaps our own language will not be used but that will be after our days."

SOURCE: Interview with Siah Hicks (Creek), November 17, 1937, *Indian-Pioneer History* (Oklahoma Historical Society), 29:80. Public domain.

MAMA AND PAPA HAVE THE GOING HOME SHIPROCK BLUES

(based on T. C. Cannon painting titles)

Song 1.
Beef Issue at Fort Sill

We were corralled then
Like horses, like captives
Like slaves. We were
Anything but horses, captives,
And slaves. But we were
hungry.

Song 2.
Two Guns Arikara

The right hand knows what the left
Hand is dreaming.
The left hand might be less sure of
The absolute world but it knows
How to follow.
Together.
We have it.

Song 3.
Soldiers

We were ready to defend the land
And the people against those
Who wanted what was not theirs to take.
We were called *heathen*
But who is *heathen* here?

Song 4.
Sioux-Soldier-Sold

There is the law of the Creator which
Tells us:
Do not take what is not yours to take.
Do not take more than you can use.
Respect life and the giver of life.
Give back.
Defend your people when there is need
For defense.
And when a people strips your spirit of
Your body and sells your "red skins" for
Bounty, then they are the ones
Who have broken the law.

Song 5.
Zero Hero

The way it is told, is we are one people
Then there was a disagreement.
Some went east. Some west.
We were bound to meet up.
We could have had a feast and helped each other.
Made an alliance.
We could have run horses together, gone hunting
For food, cooked, and stayed up sharing stories
About where we came from and where we are going:
Together.

Song 6.
Let 'Em Eat Grass

What we speak always returns
With a spike of barbs
Or the sweet taste of berries in summer.

Song 7.
Three Ghost Figures

The Past rose up before us and cried
In the voices of the children who were dragged
To Indian school and never returned.
The Present spoke up and those who remembered
How to listen could hear.
We offered tobacco and paid attention
To their stories.
The Future was a path through soldiers
With Gatling guns and GMO spoiled crops
Motioning us to safety.

Song 8.

All the Tired Horses in the Sun and **Waiting Indians
in Hospital**

Forever.

And ever.

And ever.

There's my cousin. Auntie. Uncle.

Another cousin.

Ever.

And ever.

And ever.

Vending machines and pop.

Chips, candy and not enough clean water.

And ever, ever, ever.

Waiting and tired.

Tired of waiting.

Forever.

And ever.

And ever.

Go water the horses.

Song 9.
It's a Good Day to Die

What a good dance
All night under the stars
Under the blanket with you
Honey.
We go home in our old *chidi*.
Must run on love
Because we can't afford gas.
Sun coming up
We give thanks to the Creator
For life, these lands
Family, how the bad is always
Followed by something good
I love you forever, honey.
A love like ours never
Dies.

My great-grandfather Monahwee (Menawa) Okfuskee, one of the
Red Stick chiefs, emigrated west along with his wife Betsy Coser
and their extended family, with Detachment 3, which started
four miles east of Talladega. This was the detachment of Upper
Creeks living along the Tallapoosa from Horseshoe Bend to
Tallassee. There were two prominent chiefs in this party. The other
was Tuscoona Harjo of Fish Pond. This party was conducted to
Indian Territory by Dr. R. W. Williams on behalf of the Alabama
Emigrating Company. They left about noon on September 17, 1836.

A few weeks before the party set out, the first English newspaper
was established in Hawaii.

The most popular songs in the country as they set foot were "The
Carrier Dove," "Corn Cobs Twist Your Hair," "The Light of Other
Days (The Maid of Artois)" and "Rory O'More."

By November they would camp twelve miles below Memphis.
Memphis was erected over Choctaw and Chickasaw territories. The
city of Memphis was founded in 1819.

HOW TO WRITE A POEM IN A TIME OF WAR

You can't begin just anywhere. It's a wreck.

Shrapnel and the eye

Of a house, a row of houses. There's a rat scrambling

From light with fleshy trash in its mouth. A baby strapped

to its mother's back, cut loose.
Soldiers crawl the city,

the river, the town, the village,

the bedroom, our kitchen. They eat everything.
Or burn it.

They kill what they cannot take. They rape. What they cannot kill
they take.
Rumors fall like rain.

Like bombs.

Like mother and father tears
swallowed for restless peace.

Like sunset slanting toward a moonless midnight.

Like a train blown free of its destination.   Like a seed

fallen where

there is no chance of trees   or anyplace   for birds to live.

No, start here.   Deer peer from the edge of the woods.

We used to see woodpeckers

the size of the sun, and were greeted

by chickadees with their good morning songs.

We'd started to cook outside, slippery with dew and laughter,

ah these smoky sweet sunrises.

We tried to pretend war wasn't going to happen.

Though they began building their houses all around us

and demanding more.

They started teaching our children their god's story,

A story in which we'd always be slaves.

No. Not here.

You can't begin here.

This is memory shredded because it is impossible to hold with words,

even poetry.

. . .

These memories were left here with the trees:

The torn pocket of your daughter's hand-sewn dress,

the sash, the lace.

The baby's delicately beaded moccasin still connected to the foot,

A young man's note of promise to his beloved—

No! This is not the best place to begin.

Everyone was asleep, despite the distant bombs.

Terror had become the familiar stranger.

Our beloved twin girls curled up in their nightgowns,

next to their father and me.

If we begin here, none of us will make it to the end

Of the poem.

Someone has to make it out alive, sang a grandfather

to his grandson, his granddaughter,

as he blew his most powerful song into the hearts of the children.

There it would be hidden from the soldiers,

Who would take them miles, rivers, mountains

from the navel cord place of the origin story.

He knew one day, far day, the grandchildren would return,

generations later over slick highways, constructed over old trails

Through walls of laws meant to hamper or destroy, over stones

bearing libraries of the winds.

He sang us back

to our home place from which we were stolen

in these smoky green hills.

Yes, begin here.

MVSKOKE MOURNING SONG

Sin-e-cha was aboard the *Monmouth*, which sank in the Mississippi
    River.
In 1937, Elsie Edwards related the following story of Sin-e-cha:

"Somewhere upon the banks of the Grand River near Fort Gibson
lies an old grave of an old lady whose name was Sin-e-cha. I
could lead you to that grave today. Sin-e-cha had come with her
tribal town of Ke-cho-ba-da-gee during the removal to the new
country. When the events, with never no more to live in the east,
had taken place, she, too, remembered that she had left her home
and with shattered happiness she carried a small bundle of her
few belongings and reopening and retying her pitiful bundle she
began a sad song which was later taken up by the others on board
the ship at the time of the wreck and the words of her song were:

"'I have no more land. I am driven away from home, driven up
the red waters, let us all go, let us all die together and somewhere
upon the banks we will be there.'"

SOURCE: Interview with Elsie Edwards, September 17, 1937,
Indian-Pioneer History (Oklahoma Historical Society), 23:255.
Public domain.

FIRST MORNING

for Shan Goshorn, December 3, 2018

This is the first morning we are without you on earth.
The sun greeted us after a week of rain
In your eastern green and mountain homelands.
Plants are fed, the river restored, and you have been woven
Into a path of embracing stars of all colors
Now free of the suffering that shapes us here.
We all learn to let go, like learning how to walk
When we first arrive here.
All those you thought you lost now circle you
And you are free of pain and heartbreak.
Don't look back, keep going.
We will carry your memory here, until we join you
In just a little while, in one blink of star time.

SINGING EVERYTHING

Once there were songs for everything,
Songs for planting, for growing, for harvesting,
For eating, getting drunk, falling asleep,
For sunrise, birth, mind-break, and war.
For death (those are the heaviest songs and they
Have to be pried from the earth with shovels of grief).
Now all we hear are falling-in-love songs and
Falling apart after falling in love songs.
The earth is leaning sideways
And a song is emerging from the floods
And fires. Urgent tendrils lift toward the sun.
You must be friends with silence to hear.
The songs of the guardians of silence are the most powerful—
They are the most rare.

FALLING FROM THE NIGHT SKY
(a song)

I was a star falling from the night sky
I needed you to catch me
I was a rainbow lifting from a dark cloud
I needed you to see me

You keep your eyes to the ground
Walk that line she had to you.
That path of patient expectation.
Keeps you true to her undoing.

My heart wore flowers and a red dress.
The first time we kissed
You smelled of happiness and moonlight
We drove the night to tenderness.

When you're here we are the sun and the moon.
In the land where promises come true.
When you're here, we share imagination
No explanations.
It's just me, and you.

You keep your eyes to the ground
Walk that line she had to you.
That path of patient expectation.
Keeps you true to her undoing.

I am a star falling from the night sky
I need you to catch me
I am a rainbow lifting from a dark cloud
I need you to see me

Our knowledge is based on the origin stories of land, genealogy and ancestors. If you know the branches of the tree of relationship between tribal clans and family members, then you know who you are, said the panther to its cubs.

FOR EARTH'S GRANDSONS

Stand tall, no matter your height, how dark your skin
Your spirit is all colors within
You are made of the finest woven light
From the iridescent love that formed your mothers, fathers
Your grandparents all the way back on the spiral road—
There is no end to this love
It has formed your bodies
Feeds your bright spirits
And no matter what happens in these times of breaking—
No matter dictators, the heartless, and liars
No matter—you are born of those
Who kept ceremonial embers burning in their hands
All through the miles of relentless exile
Those who sang the path through massacre
All the way to sunrise
You will make it through—

RUNNING

It's closing time. Violence is my boyfriend
With a cross to bear
                        Hoisted on by the church.
He wears it everywhere.
There are no female deities in the Trinity.
            I don't know how I'm going to get out of here,
Said the flying fish to the tree.
                        Last call.
We've had it with history, we who look for vision here
In the Indian and poetry bar, somewhere
To the left of Hell.
Now I have to find my way, when there's a river to cross and no
Boat to get me there, when there appears to be no home at all.
                        My father gone, chased
By the stepfather's gun. *Get out of here.*
I've found my father at the bar, his ghost at least, some piece
Of him in this sorry place. The boyfriend's convincing to a crowd.
Right now, he's the spell of attraction. What tales he tells.
In the fog of thin hope, I wander this sad world
We've made with the enemy's words.
The lights quiver,
    Like they do when the power's dwindling to a dangling string.
It is time to go home. We are herded like stoned cattle, like
    children for the bombing drill—
            Out the door, into the dark street of this old Indian town
Where *there are no Indians anymore.*
I was afraid of the dark because then I could see
                        Everything. The truth with its eyes staring
Back at me. The mouth of the dark with its shiny moon teeth,
No words, just a hiss and a snap.

I could hear my heart hurting
With my *in-the-dark* ears.
I thought I could take it. Where was the party?
It's been a century since we left home with the American soldiers
    at our backs.
The party had long started up in the parking lot.
He flew through the dark, broke my stride with a punch.
I went down then came up.
I thought I could take being a girl with her heart in her
Arms. I carried it for justice. For the rights of all Indians.
We all had that cross to bear.
Those Old Ones followed me, the quiet girl with the long dark hair,
The daughter of a warrior who wouldn't give up.
I wasn't ready yet, to fling free the cross

I ran and I ran through the 2 A.M. streets.

It was my way of breaking free. I was anything but history.
I was the wind.

A REFUGE IN THE SMALLEST OF PLACES

For Emily Dickinson, one of the singers.
And for all who those fleeing on those ancient migration
trails north, for home.

Someone sang for me and no one else could hear it
When I had given up and made knife marks on my arm
Or drank and gave myself away or was given

Someone sang for me and no one else could hear it
When demons came with rope and cages
To take my children from me and imprison us

Someone sang for me and no one else could hear it
Now I am here in the timeless room of lost poetry
Gathering up the destroyed and forgotten
Because of the songs someone sang that no one else could hear

But me.

I'M NOBODY! WHO ARE YOU?
Emily Dickinson

I'm Nobody! Who are you?
Are you – Nobody – too?
Then there's a pair of us!
Don't tell! they'd advertise – you know!

How dreary – to be – Somebody!
How public – like a Frog –
To tell one's name – the livelong June –
To an admiring Bog!

Emily Dickinson was six years old when Monahwee and his family began the emigration to the West.

BOURBON AND BLUES

for T. C. Cannon, a brother of poetry and song

We were wild then,
As we emerged from bloody history
Into the white clothes of pious religion and rules.
Then sent off to Indian school to learn how to forget
Our mothers, fathers, the grandparents who loved and love us.
We were still in the embrace of the God of the plains,
Horses, of where sky and earth meet—
Every day was a praise song, every word or act had import
Into the meaning of why we are here as spirits
Dressed in colored earth.

We were wild then,
They said, because we spoke a different language
And would not give over our spirits to them.
And though they tried, they could not ever remake us
No matter how hard they drilled and forced us.
We died over and over again in those stiff desks,
As our hearts walked home.
We sat on the fire escapes outside our dorm rooms on cold winter nights
And made plans to escape history.

We were wild then.
We didn't take well to mind imprisonment.
Our dreams could not be confined by the walls of institutional green
of misbegotten bureaucracy.
We found alcohol, smoke and anything else to *break on through to
    the other side*
Where our visions shivered there near the hills outside of campus,
waiting for us to recover from the sickness of forgetfulness.

. . .

Some of us did not make it.
We carried their bodies far away
From the cities and set their spirits free.
This moment is for them—gives them nourishment
Of our love to keep moving toward home.

We were wild then.
I will always remember that night far south
Of town where we sat at the bar after our escape.
You had gone to war and had become a painter, poet and singer.
I was a poet, mother and I was learning how to sing.
We talked history, heartache, the blues, and what it means
To be an artist with nothing to lose, because we lost everything,
here, at the edge of America.

MY GREAT-AUNT ELLA MONAHWEE JACOBS'S TESTIMONY

"About this time (in the early 1880s), a white man was murdered near Okfuskee Town and Grandfather Monahwee had been accused. McIntosh was afraid to attack him, for Grandfather Monahwee was second Chief of the Creeks and had a reputation for valor and military skill and was always known to be the leader when danger threatened. Grandfather was also a doctor of medicine and at all times he would have gourds tied around his waist filled with different kinds of herbs for his medicines."

ROAD

We stand first in our minds, and then we toddle
From hand to furniture
Soon we are walking away from the house and lands
Of our ancestral creator gods
To the circles of friends, of schooling, of work
Making families and worlds of our own.
We make our way through storm and sun
We walk side by side or against each other
The last road will be taken alone—
There might be crowds calling for blood
Or a curtained window by the leaving bed
It is best to not be afraid
Lift your attention
For the appearance of the next road
It might be through a family of trees, a desert, or
On rolling waves of sea
It's the ancient road the soul knows
We always remember it when we see it
It beckons at birth
It carries us home

The Southeast was covered with Mississippian mound builder cities and communities a century before Spanish arrival in the Southeast. The Southeast is still covered with the remains of mounds. There are even mounds on the University of Tennessee, Knoxville campus. These mounds might be leveled by shovels, tractors or hate, but they will show up on any energetic geophysical map. They continue to exist in memory, in memory maps.

It is said that Monahwee got his warrior name Hopothepoya (Crazy War Hunter) from stealing horses in Knoxville. Knoxville was in traditional Mvskoke territory, therefore, the horses were not technically stolen. They were on stolen lands.

When I returned to these homelands I came by old trails. One of the most traveled trails is part of Interstate 40.

DESIRE'S DOG

I was desire's dog.
I ate when I was fed. I did what I was told.
I knew how to sit, stand and roll over on command.
When I was petted, I was made whole.
Even when I dreamed, I dreamed a chain around my neck.

Desire is a bone with traces of fat.
It's the wag smell of a bitch in heat.
It's that pinched hit at the end of a beat.
It's a stick thrown into a rabbit chase.

I lay at the feet of desire for years.

Then I heard this song, calling me.
It was a woman in a red dress,
It was a man with a gun in his hand.
It was a table filled with fruit and flowers.
It was a fox of fire, a bird of stone.

Then, it was gone.

What was left disintegrated by rain and wind.

I had followed desire, to the end.

DAWNING

Even the birds were still sleeping
When I touched ground.
I went around the house, opening
Windows, then the plants.
Made my tea, wrote until breaking
Of morning. I went back
Up the stairs to see if you were waking.
Ever so quiet the smoky light
Covered the hills, no one making
The rounds yet to pick up trash
Or edge the grass. You were dreaming
When I cradled your head.
Your mother's loving
Tenderly in place though she's been gone
For many years, and you graying
Though ever handsome
In my arms. I tiptoe back to the breaking
Of light and let you sleep—
My king, my everything.

HONORING

Who sings to the plants
That are grown for our plates?
Are they gathered lovingly
In aprons or arms?
Or do they suffer the fate
Of the motor-driven whip
Of the monster reaper?
No song at all, only
The sound of money
Being stacked in a bank
Who stitched the seams in my clothes
One line after another?
Was the room sweaty and dark
With no hour to spare?
Did she have enough to eat?
Did she have a home anywhere?
Or did she live on the floor?
And where were the children?
Or was the seamstress the child
With no home of his or her own?
Who sacrifices to make clothes
For strangers of another country?
And why?
Let's remember to thank the grower of food
The picker, the driver,
The sun and the rain.
Let's remember to thank each maker of stitch
And layer of pattern,
The dyer of color
In the immense house of beauty and pain.

.   .   .

Let's honor the maker.
Let's honor what's made.

MY MAN'S FEET

They are heroic roots
You cannot mistake them
For any other six-foot walker
I could find them in a sea of feet
A planet or universe of feet

They kicked the sky at birth
In that town his great-grandfather found
My man's feet left childhood
Past the mineral grit of an oil flush bust
To these atomic eastbound lands

His feet are made of his mother's spiritual concern
And of his father: historic, and mindfully upright
What walkers—
From mound builder steps that led to the sky maker
Past Spanish galleons, stage coach, and railroad snaker

One generation following another
No other feet but these could bare
The rock stubborn loyal bear
Towering intelligence and children picker upper
That is the one who owns these feet

What an anchor his feet provide
For his unmatched
Immensability and get up againality

I've danced behind this man in the stomp dance circle.
Our feet beating rhythm together
Man, woman, boy, girl, sun and moon jumper.

. . .

My man's feet are the sure steps of a father
Looking after his sons, his daughters
For when he laughs he opens all the doors of our hearts
Even as he forgets to shut them when he leaves

And when he grieves for those he loves
He carves out valleys enough to hold everyone's tears
With his feet, these feet
My man's widely humble, ever steady, beautiful brown feet.

"I WONDER WHAT YOU ARE THINKING,"

The feathered wife asked her feathered husband—

She watches as he cleans his wings, notes how he sends his eyes
    over the horizon
To viridian in the flying away direction.
So many migrations stacked within sky memory.

Her body is stirring with eggs. She tucks found materials
Into their nest with her beak.
The nerves in her wingtips sense rains coming to soften the ground.
To send food to the surface of earth.

He says nothing—
As he wonders about the careless debris that humans make
Even as it yields ribbon, floss and string.

Housecats and their sporting trails are on his mind's map.
There are too many in this neighborhood.

A ragged yellow fellow eats birds after hours of play.
He stays out of that tom's way, and has warned his wife
The same. Though she's more wisely wary than him.

Dogs are easy. They bark and leap and wag their tails.
They have no concerns for most flying things.
They lap up human trails for love.

And why do we keep renewing this ceremony of nests?
Each feathered generation flies away.
What does it mean, and why
the green growing green

turning red against yellow,
then gray, gray and green again?

When I need her heartbeat
In the freeze winds why is she always there
And not somewhere else?

Her lilt question has made an echo in his ears
like a string fluttering from a bush
In a delicate spring wind:

I wonder what you are thinking . . .

He doesn't answer.

Then he does.

"Nothing.
I was thinking about the nothing of nothing at all."

FOR THOSE WHO WOULD GOVERN

First question: Can you first govern yourself?

Second question: What is the state of your own household?

Third question: Do you have a proven record of community service and compassionate acts?

Fourth question: Do you know the history and laws of your principalities?

Fifth question: Do you follow sound principles? Look for fresh vision to lift all the inhabitants of the land, including animals, plants, elements, all who share this earth?

Sixth question: Are you owned by lawyers, bankers, insurance agents, lobbyists, or other politicians, anyone else who would unfairly profit by your decisions?

Seventh question: Do you have authority by the original keepers of the lands, those who obey natural law and are in the service of the lands on which you stand?

RABBIT INVENTS THE SAXOPHONE

When one of the last trails of tears wound through New Orleans
Rabbit, that ragged trickster, decided he wanted
To be a musician. He was tired of walking. And they had all the fun.
They got all the women, they were surrounded
By fans who gave them smokes, drinks, and he could have
All kinds of friends to do his bidding.
But, Rabbit hadn't proved to be musical.
When he led at stomp dance no one would follow.
No shell shaker would shake shells for him.
He was never invited to lead, even when the young ones
Were called up to practice.

The first thing a musician needs is a band, he said to his friends.
The hottest new music was being made at Congo Square—
So many tribes were jamming there: African, Native, and a few
    remnant French.
Making a new music of melody, love and beat.

Rabbit climbed up to the stage but had nothing to offer.
Just his strut, charming banter, and what looked like a long stick
Down the tight leg of pants.

Musicians are musicians, no trick will get by.
You either have it, or want it
Nothing else will fly.

Do you know any songs?
What can you play?
Can you sing?
Do you have a piano, tuba, or strings?

. . .

The musicians began vamping,
What can this Rabbit cat do?
Is he going to blow hot air
Or fart in the rain?

Rabbit turned his back to the band
Like that genius Miles Davis
Pulled out his stick
He made a horn with his hands.

This stick is so special, bragged Rabbit.
As he turned back to the jam
No one else has one like this.
You've never heard it before.
It's called a sax-oh-oh-phone.

Rabbit's newborn horn made a rip in the sky
It made old women dance, and girls fall to their knees
It made singers of tricksters, it made tricksters of players
It made trouble wherever it sang after that—

The last time we heard Rabbit was for my cousin's run for chief.
There was a huge feed. Everyone showed up to eat.
Rabbit's band got down after the speeches.
We danced through the night, and nobody fought.
Nor did anyone show up the next day to vote.
They were sleeping.

When Adolfe Sax patented the first saxophone on June 23, 1846, the Creek Nation was in turmoil. The people had been moved west of the Mississippi River after the Creek Wars which culminated in the Battle of Horseshoe Bend. We were putting our lives back together in new lands where we were promised we would be left alone. The saxophone made it across the big waters and was introduced in brass bands in the South. The music followed rivers into new towns, cities, all the way to our new lands. Not long after, in the early 1900s, my grandmother Naomi Harjo learned to play saxophone. I can feel her now when I play the instrument we both loved and love. The saxophone is so human. Its tendency is to be rowdy, edgy, talk too loud, bump into people, say the wrong words at the wrong time, but then, you take a breath all the way from the center of the earth and blow. All that heartache is forgiven. All that love we humans carry makes a sweet, deep sound and we fly a little.

LET THERE BE NO REGRETS

for Bears Ears National Monument

We're not losing the birch trees, the birch trees are losing us.

—WAYNE "MINOGIIZHIG" VALLIERE

The songs and stories that formed us are restless
and need a place to live in the world of our grandchildren.
They are weary with waiting.

Earth continues to dream her earth dreams
Though desperate thoughts fed by money hunger roam our minds.

To the destroyers, Earth is not a person.

They will want more until there is no more to steal.

Earth who does not know time is patient.
The destroyers will destroy themselves.

So many earth spirits take care of this place. They emerge from
the cliff walls.
They emerge from the waves of waters.

Our ancestors are not only human ancestors.
What do you see when you fly to the top of the ancestor tree?

Let there be no regrets, no sadness, no anger, no acts of
disturbance to these lands.

ADVICE FOR COUNTRIES, ADVANCED, DEVELOPING AND FALLING

A CALL AND RESPONSE

A country is a person.

A country is a noun, to be bought and sold. I have a deed.

The ruler's disposition and rules determine the state of being for
    all constituents.

*Each state governs itself without respect for individuals. It's everyone
    for themselves.*

Power is dangerous when wielded in the hands of one. It is meant
    to be shared.

*I was given this position by cunning, by money, by sex, by family, by God.
    It belongs to me and no one else.*

We cannot own anyone else, people, the lands, or resources. We
    are here to care for each other.

*We are right. We build walls to keep anyone who is not like us out of
    here. God gave us these lands. We separate children and cage them
    because they are breaking our God's law.*

. . .

Every increment of any thought, action, or deed matters, has
    consequences in all directions.

*Not if you can make a law. Not if it passes the Supreme Court. Not if we
can pay for it.*

There will be no balance without all voices present in the power circle.

*You will never earn your way here. You are the wrong sex, wrong color of
skin, wrong sexual orientation, not my religion, not my language.*

We are making our grandchildren's world with our words. We
    perceive a world in which everyone sits at the table together,
    with enough for everyone.

"We will make this country great again."

TOBACCO ORIGIN STORY

It was way back, before there was a way back
When time threaded earth and sky
Children were conceived, were born, grew, and walked tall
In what we now call a day.
Every planted thought grew plant
Ladders to the stars, way back, before there was
No way back, *Miss Mary Mack*
We used to sing along the buttons of her
Dress. Our babies are always
Our babies. Even back then when time waved through
The corn. We knew our plants like
Relatives. Their stories were our stories, there
Were songs for everything then,
for every transformation
From that first couple, a young Mvskoke man
And woman, who walked through the
shimmer of the early evening.
They had become as one song.
They lay down when it was dark. I can hear their
Intimate low-voice talking
How they tease each other with such gut love.
Earth makes a bed, with pillow
Mounds. And it is there as the night insects sing
They conceived their first child. They
Will look back as they walk east toward the sunrise
The raw stalks of beginning
Will drink the light, root deeply dark into earth.
In the tracks of their loving
The plant child emerges, first the seed head, then
Leafy, long male body and the white female

Flowers of tobacco, or
Hece, as the people called it when it called
To them. *Come here. We were brought*
To you from those who love you. We will help you.
And that's how it began, way
Back, when we knew how to hear the songs of plants
And could sing back, like now
On paper, with marks like bird feet, but where are
Our ears? They have grown to fit
Around earbuds, to hear music made for cold
Cash, like our beloved smoke
Making threaded with addiction and dead words.
Sing this song back to me girl.
In the moonlight tobacco plant had silver
Moon buttons all up her back.
We're getting dressed to go plant new songs with words.
Our sun is dimming faster.
Mvto hece, mvto hvse, mvto—
Ekvnvchaga, mvto ah

My aunt Lois Harjo told me that our grandfather Monahwee had to go into hiding once, after removal to Indian Territory. When he came upon a white man beating his wife in the street, he took the whip from the husband's hand and beat him. The government agents of law enforcement in Okmulgee looked for Monahwee to charge him with a crime, but he hid out in the pockets of Native communities that white men didn't enter.

Monahwee is buried near Eufaula, Oklahoma, in a small Creek Indian family cemetery. His unmarked gravesite is surrounded by seven cedar trees. My cousin John Scott, known as "Porky," showed me his burial place.

REDBIRD LOVE

We watched her grow up.
She was the urgent chirper,
Fledgling flier.
And when spring rolled
Out its green
She'd grown
Into the most noticeable
Bird-girl.
Long-legged and just
The right amount of blush
Tipping her wings, crest
And tail, and
She knew it
In the bird parade.
We watched her strut.
She owned her stuff.
The males perked their armor, greased their wings,
And flew sky-loop missions
To show off
For her.
In the end
There was only one.
There's that one you circle back to—for home.
This morning
The young couple scavenge seeds
On the patio.
She is thickening with eggs.
Their minds are busy with sticks the perfect size, tufts of fluff
Like dandelion, and other pieces of soft.
He steps aside for her, so she can eat.

Then we watch him fill his beak
Walk tenderly to her and kiss her with seed.
The sacred world lifts up its head
To notice—
We are double, triple blessed.

We follow the DNA spiral of stories from dawn to dusk, from night dance to sunrise. Once I was brought into the memory of the Battle of Horseshoe Bend by time. Time rides the spiral with wild precision. When I got there with time in time, the earthworks planted for defense of heavy logs had been broken through by Andrew Jackson's troops. In the hellish fire and smoke of battle, we could not keep hold of the front line. We were no match for their numbers, their guns, their cannons. Time in these lands as we knew it was over and we fought the intruders and the terrible weight of knowing with everything in us. My grandfather Monahwee was shot seven times, and when Jackson's troops pronounced victory and retreated, he crawled to the edge of the Tallapoosa River and rolled into the bloody current as soldiers bayoneted the dead and stole booty. My grandfather's life force curled into his belly. I felt the giving away to history which in no means meant giving up. For a warrior it is not possible to give up. I smelled suffering and tasted the metallic wash of blood, of loss in my mouth. Many of us lay dead and wounded. Through the immense and terrible echo of injustice a meadow bird sang and sang.

BECOMING SEVENTY
for Marilyn Kallet

We

arrived

when the days

grew legs of night—

Chocolates were offered

We ate latkes for hours

To celebrate light and friends—

We will keep going despite dark

Or a madman in a white house dream.

Let's talk about something else said the dog

Who begs faithfully at the door of good will:

A biscuit will do, a voice of reason, meat sticks—

I dreamed all of this I told her, you, me, and Paris—

It was impossible to make it through the tragedy

Without poetry. What are we without winds becoming words?

. . .

Becoming old children born to children born to sing us into

Love. Another level of love, beyond the neighbor's holiday light

Display proclaiming goodwill to all men who have lost their way in the dark

As they tried to find the car door, the bottle hidden behind the seat, reason

To keep on going past all the times they failed at sharing love, love. It's weak they think—

Or some romantic bullshit, a movie set propped up behind on slats, said the wizard

Of junk understanding who pretends to be the wise all-knowing dog behind a cheap fan—

It's in the plan for the new world straining to break through the floor of this one, said the Angel of—

All-That-You-Know-And-Forgot-And-Will-Find, as she flutters at the edge of your mind when you try hard—

Sing the blues to the future of everything that might happen and will. All the losses come tumbling—

Down, down, down at three in the morning as do all the shouldn't haves or should haves. It doesn't matter, girl, girl—

I'll be here to pick you up, said Memory, in her red shoes, and the dress that showed off brown legs. When you first met

.   .   .

Him at the age you have always loved, hair perfect with a little wave,
and that shine in your skin from believing that—

Impossible was possible, you were not afraid. You stood up in love in
a French story and there fell ever, eve—

A light rain as you crossed the Seine to meet him for café in St.
Germaine de Pres. You wrote a poem beneath the tender moon—

Skin from your ribs to your hip bone, in the slender then, and you are
still writing that song to convince the sweetness of every

Bit of straggling moonlight, star and sunlight to become words in
your mouth, in your kiss—that kiss that will never die, you will
always fall—

fall way in love. It doesn't matter how old, how many days, hours, or
memories, we can fall in love over and over and then—

again. The Seine or Tennessee or any river with a soul knows the depths
descending when it comes to seeing the sun or moon stare stars—

Back, without shame, remorse, or guilt. This is what I remember she
told her husband when they bedded down that night in the house
that would begin their

Marriage. That house was built of twenty-four doves, rugs from
India, cooking recipes from seven generations of mother, hope, and
their sisters,

And wave upon wave of tears, and the concrete of resolution for the
steps that continue all the way to the heavens, past guardian lion
dogs, dog

. . .

After dog to protect. They are humble earth angels, and the rowdiest, even nasty. You try and lick yourself like that, imagine. And the shrewd Old

Woman laughed as she slipped off her cheap shoes and parked them under the bed that lay at the center of the garden of good and evil. She'd seen it all. Done it much

More than once. Tonight, she just wanted a good sleep, and picked up the book of poetry by her bed, which was over a journal she kept when her mother was dying.

These words from May Sarton she kept in the fourth room of her heart, "Love, come upon him warily and deep / For if he startle first it were as well / to bind a fox's throat

With a gold bell / As hold him when it is his will to leap. . . ." And she considered that every line of a poem was a lead line into the spirit world to capture a bit of

Memory, pieces of gold confetti, a kind of celebration. We all want to be remembered, even memory, even the way the light came on bright in the kitchen

Window, when her mother turned up the dial on that cool mist color of a radio, when memory crossed the path of longing and took mother's arm and she put down her apron

Said, "I don't mind if I do," and they danced, you watching, as you began your own cache of remembering. Already you had stored the taste of mother as sweet milk, father as a labor

. . .

Of sweat and love, and night as a lonely boat of stars that took you
into who you were before you slid through the hips of the story.
There are no words when you cross the rippling skin of the

Gate of forbidden waters, or is it a sheer scarf of the finest silk,
or is it something else that causes you to forget. Nothing is ever
forgotten says the god of remembering

who protects the heartbeat of every little cell of knowing from the
Antarctic to the soft spot at the top of this planetary baby. Oh
baby, come here, hear, let me tell you the story

of the party you will never forget, no matter where you go, where
you are, or where you will be when you cross the line and say, no
more. No more greedy kings, no more disappointments, no more
orphans, no—

or thefts of souls or lands, no more killing for the sport of killing.
No more, no more, except more of the story so I will understand
exactly what I am doing here, and why, she said to the red fox

guardian who took her arm to help her cross the road that was
given to the care of Natives who made sure the earth spirits were
fed with songs, and the other things they loved to eat. They like
sweets, cookies, salt and flowers.

It was getting late and the fox guardian picked up her books as
she hurried through the streets of strife. But it wasn't getting late.
There was no late, only a plate of tamales on the counter waiting
to be, or

. . .

Not to be. At this age, said the fox, we are closer to the not to
be, which is the to be in the fields of sweet grasses. Wherever
you are, enjoy the evening, how the sun walks the horizon before
crossing grief—

Over to be, and we then exist under the realm of the water moon.
There's where fears slay us, in the dark of the howling mind. We
all battle. Befriend them, the moon said as a crab skittered under
her skirt, her daughter in

the high chair, waiting for cereal and toast. What a girl she turned
out to be, a willow tree, a blessing to the winds, to her family.
There she is married, and we start the story all over again, said her
proud father

in a toast to the happiness of who we are and who we are becoming
as slick change in a new model sedan whips it down the freeway
toward the generations that follow, one after another in the original

lands of the Cherokees who are still here. Nobody goes anywhere
though we are always leaving and returning. It's a ceremony.
Sunrise occurs everywhere, in lizard time, human time, or a fern
uncurling time. When dark—

we instinctually reach for light food, we digest it, make love, art
or trouble. The sun crowns us at noon. The whole earth is a queen.
At sunset say goodbye to hurt, to suffering, goodbye to the pain
you caused others. Good bye, bye, don't cry.

Goodbye, goodbye, to Carrie Fisher, the Star Wars phenomenon,
and George Michael the singer. They were planets in our genera-
tional emotional universe. Some of my memories pin to a minute
of love on a big screen in an

. . .

imagined future, or broken open when the sax solo of "Careless Whisper" blows through the communal heart. Yes, there's a cosmic consciousness. Jung named it but it was there long before named by Vedic and Mvskoke scientists. And, there breathes stars here—

a cosmic hearteousness—the heart is the higher mind and nothing can be forgotten there, no ever or ever. How do I sing this so I don't forget? Ask the poets. Each word is a box that can be opened or closed. Then trains of words, or phrases

garnered by music and the need for rhythm to organize chaos. Like right, now, in this poem is the transition phase. I remember it while giving birth, summer sun bearing down on the city melting asphalt but there we were, my daughter and I,

at the door between worlds. I was happier than ever before to welcome her, happiness was the path she chose to enter, and I couldn't push yet, not yet, and then there appeared a pool of the bluest water. We waited there for a breath: one, two, three, four

to catch up, and then it did, and she took it that girl who was beautiful beyond dolphin dreaming, and we made it, we did, to the other side of suffering. This is the story our mothers tell but we couldn't hear it in our ears stuffed with junk advertising,

with our mothers' own loathing set in place by patriarchal scripture, the smothering rules to stop insurrection by domesticated slaves . . . wives. It hurt everybody's song. The fathers cannot know what they are feeling in such a spiritual backwash. Worship

boxes set into place by the need for money and power will not beget freedom. Only war ships. For freedom, freedom, oh freedom sang the slaves, the oar rhythm of the blues lifting up the spirits of our peoples whose bodies were worn out, or destroyed by a man's slash

hit of greed. This is our memory too, said America. Heredity is a field of blood, celebration, and forgetfulness. Don't take on more than you can carry, said the eagle to his twin sons, fighting each other in the sky over a fox, dangling between them.

It's that time of the year, when we eat tamales and latkes. We light candles, make fires to make the way for a newborn child, for fresh understanding. Demons will try to make houses out of jealousy, anger, pride, greed, or more destructive material. They place them in a cracked part

of the body that will hold them: liver, heart, knee, or brain. So, my friend, let's let that go, for joy, for chocolates made of ashes, mangos, grapefruit, or chili from Oaxaca, for sparkling wine from Spain, for these children who show up in our dreams and want to live at any cost because life says

we are here to feed them joy. Your soul so finely woven the silk-worms went on strike, said the mulberry tree. We all have mul-berry trees in the memory yard. They hold the place for skinned knees earned by small braveries, cousins you love who are gone. All memory bends to fit. We become poems.

BEYOND

Beyond sunrise, there is a song we follow
Beyond clouds traveling with rain humped
On their backs, lightning in their fists
Beyond the blue horizon where our ancestors
Appear bearing gifts, wrapped in blankets woven
With sun and strands of scarlet time

Beyond the footpaths we walk every day
From sunrise to kitchen, to work, to garden, to play
To sunset, to dark, and back

Beyond where the baby sleeps, her breath
A light mist of happiness making
A fine rainbow of *becoming knowledgeable* around us

Beyond the children learning alphabets
And numbers, bent over their sticks and dolls
As they play war and family, grow human paths

Beyond the grandmothers and grandfathers
Their mothers and fathers, and in the marrow of their bones
To when that song was first sung we traveled on

Beyond sunset, can you hear it?
The shaking of shells, the drumming of feet, the singers
Singing, all of us, all at once?

In the song of beyond, how deep we are—

REN-TOH-PVRV

TRANSLATION OF "BEYOND"

*Hvs-os-sv ren-toh-pv-rv, v-ho-lo-ce hvl-we ful-lat os-ke a-ce-koh-yet
mon v-tok-yv-hat-en no-kof-ti-cet ho-yan-e-cof pom yv-hi-ke-tv po-hēt
a-cak-a-pē-yēs*

*Su-tv ces-kv ho-lat-ten ren-toh-pv-rv, pom v-cul-v-ke em-kv o-ke-tv mon
v-ce-tv he-ra-kat a-pvl-la-pi-cet es-yi-ces*

*Ne-ne v-pas-ku-ce ren-to-pv-rv, hvs-os-sv o-ke-tv, hom-pe-tv-cu-ko,
v-tot-ke-tv, cv-po-fv, ak-ko-pvn-kv, mon hvs-ak-lat-kv o-ke-tv, no-ci-cet,
o-ke-tv hv-tvm te-re-pot-a-ran-es*

*Ho-pue-wv no-cat ren-toh-pv-rv, en he-sa-ke-tv cvm-po-se a-fvc-ke
ha-yat, nak-ker-rat po-fe-ken ce-la-yes*

*Ho-pue-ta-ke po-na-kv en-yo-lvn-kv ker-ra-kat ren-toh-pv-rv, 'to-lv-
cu-ce, es-te-v-ha-ke sa-ko-pvn-ak-es. Hor-re ha-ya-ket, cu-ko-ha-yak-et,
ah-ko-pvn-ak-es. Em po-ya-fek-cv nen-'o-ce oh-li-ca-kes*

*E-pu-se, e-pu-ca, ec-ke, er-ke, mon fo-ne en-fo-lo-wv ren-toh-pv-rv,
en-hv-te-ces-kv pom yv-hi-ke-tv yv-hi-kēt a-pe-yēs*

*Hv-sak-lat-kv ren-toh-pv-rv nak mak-a-kat po-hec-kv? Lu-cv so-pan-
vl-ke, o-pan-vl-ke, yv-hik-vl-ke o-mvl-kv e-te-hvm-ku-se yv-hi-ka-kat
po-hec-kv?*

*E-kvn-v mon su-tv em-o-pu-nvk-v, en-yv-hi-ke-tv, suf-ke-tos. Yv-hik-
e-tv ren-toh-pv-rv, pom-eu, suf-ke po-ni-yēt, yv-hik-ēs*

MEMORY SACK

That first cry opens the earth door.
We join the ancestor road.
With our pack of memories
Slung slack on our backs
We venture into the circle
Of destruction,
Which is the circle
Of creation
And make more—

Every night during the summer and into early fall here in the homelands, there is a huge concert of the insect orchestra. Now the orchestra is shutting down for the season. Last night I heard two or three stragglers trying to carry on a song. They reminded me of the last remaining souls at a forty-nine dance, bleary-eyed, dragging blankets, and still singing though everyone else has gone home.

CEHOTOSAKVTES

It is said that two beloved women sang this song as their band came over on the Trail of Tears. One woman walked near the front of the people, and the other walked near the back with the small children. When anyone faltered, they would sing this song to hold them up.

> *Cehotosakvtes*
> *Chenaorakvtes Momis komet*
> *Awatchken ohapeyakares hvlwen*

> Do not get tired.
> Don't be discouraged. Be determined.
> Come. Together let's go toward the highest place.

One March a few years back, I was in residence at a private women's college in Atlanta. I'd heard of a gathering to be held at the Battle of Horseshoe Bend grounds, which is not far from Opelika, Alabama. Many from our Muscogee Creek Nation were being bused in from Oklahoma. I wanted to see family and friends, and to once again visit homeland territory. I took a few students with me. It was a strange set of events, positioned on the anniversary of the battle which was essentially a massacre. We Mvskoke citizens came to acknowledge that we are very present in the continuum of time, and to give honor to our ancestors. That battle did not destroy us. We tribal descendants danced, spoke, visited, and some people had booths demonstrating culture and arts. Euro-American reenactors and descendants dressed up in military uniforms, paraded guns and shot off cannons. They were preparing for a reenactment of the killing. Late afternoon I drove the students back to their campus in Atlanta. They quickly dozed in the backseat as I wound through the back roads to catch the main highway to Atlanta. I noted a sign "90 miles to Atlanta." Then I heard the rhythm sound of a running horse coming up behind me. I smelled the sweat of human and horse, and as the breathy team caught up I saw my grandfather astride the horse. What a rider he was, just as I had been told in all the stories. I remembered that my aunt Lois Harjo told me how Monahwee could bend time. He could arrive at a destination on horseback long before it was physically possible. And as quickly as he'd come, he was gone, and I saw a traffic sign "30 miles to Atlanta." I'd only been on that road for a few minutes. My grandfather had come back to show me how he folded time. The Old Ones will always tell you, your ancestors keep watch over you. Listen to them.

BY THE WAY
for Adrienne Rich

I've given it time, as if time were mine to give.
There was a dam, larger than Hoover or the president or the patent
For the metal creature that sucks up all the dust.
Words had to stop and ask permission before crossing over.
Oh, sometimes they were wild with the urgency of sweet
And leaped—
Mostly the rest were kept in the net
Of swallowed, or forbidden language.

I want to go back and rewrite all the letters.
I lied frequently.
No. I was not okay.
And neither was James Baldwin though his essays
Were perfect spinning platters of comprehension of the fight
To assert humanness in a black and white world.

That's how blues emerged, by the way—
Our spirits needed a way to dance through the heavy mess.
The music, a sack that carries the bones of those left alongside
The trail of tears when we were forced
To leave everything we knew by the way—

I constructed an individual life in the so-called *civilized* world.
We all did—far from the trees and plants
Who had born us and fed us.
All I wanted was the music, I would tell you now—
Within it, what we cannot carry.
I talk about then from a hotel room just miles
From your home in the east
Before you fled on your personal path of tears

To the west, that worn-out American Dream
Dogging your steps.

You lived on a pedestal for me then, the driven diver who climbed
Back up from the abyss, Venus on a seashell with a dagger
In her hands.
I had to look, and followed your tracks in the poems
Cut by suffering.
Aren't they all?
We're in the apocalyptic age of addiction and forgetting.
It's worse now.

But that dam, I had to tell you. I broke it open stone by stone.
It took a saxophone, flowers, and your words
Had something to do with it
I can't say exactly how.
The trajectory wasn't clean even though it was sure.
Does that make sense?
Maybe it does only in the precincts of dreams and poetry,
Not in a country lit for twenty-four hours a day to keep dreams
    stuck
Turning in a wheel
In the houses of money.

I read about transcendence, how the light
Came in through the window of a nearby traveler
And every cell of creation opened its mouth
To drink grace

That's what I never told you.

When we made it down last year to the Chattahoochee River dividing Columbus and Phenix, to the Tie Snake place in the river, to the place women sang, joked and gossiped as we washed clothes, to the old tribal town sites, to where even one of our stolen houses belonging to an uncle was still standing . . .

No one had told us how beautiful it was:

the waters of this river, these healing plants, these stones, these winds roaming through on sunlight and rains, all the suns of our lost days.

They couldn't remember because to remember would have killed us when nothing else did.

WELCOMING SONG
(taught me by my cousin Joe Sulphur)

ALLAY NA LEE NO ar-ri-no (while I go/came?)

HETHLEE KNEE TOOK KAH LAY he-reen e-to-kvl-ik-en
(very well we gathered)

ALLAY NA LEE NO ar-ri-no

HOBANEEE HOBANEE E o-pan-e o-pa-ne *(dancing, dancing)*

ALLAY NA LEE NO ar-ri-no

AH JAH LUHGEE MAH GUN GHEE v-cul-a-ke mah kvn ke
(the old ones said/foretold)

ALLAY NA LEE NO   ar-ri-no

HAYOUNG GEE (G)O LEE hv-yom-e ful-le *(this way they/we go
about)*

AN AMERICAN SUNRISE

We were running out of breath, as we ran out to meet ourselves, We
Were surfacing the edge of our ancestors' fights, and ready to Strike
It was difficult to lose days in the Indian bar if you were Straight.
Easy if you played pool and drank to remember to forget. We
Made plans to be professional—and did. And some of us could Sing
When we drove to the edge of the mountains, with a drum. We
Made sense of our beautiful crazed lives under the starry stars. Sin
Was invented by the Christians, as was the Devil, we sang. We
Were the heathens, but needed to be saved from them: Thin
Chance. We knew we were all related in this story, a little Gin
Will clarify the dark, and make us all feel like dancing. We
Had something to do with the origins of blues and jazz
I argued with the music as I filled the jukebox with dimes in June,

Forty years later and we still want justice. We are still America. We.

BLESS THIS LAND

Bless this land from the top of its head to the bottom of its feet

From the arctic old white head to the brown feet of tropical rain

Bless the eyes of this land, for they witness cruelty and kindness in
this land

From sunrise light upright to falling down on your knees night

Bless the ears of this land, for they hear cries of heartbreak and
shouts of celebration in this land

*Once we heard no gunshot on these lands; the trees and stones can
be heard singing*

Bless the mouth, lips and speech of this land, for the land is a
speaker, a singer, a keeper of all that happens here, on this
land

*Luminous forests, oceans, and rock cliff sold for the trash glut of
gold, uranium, or oil bust rush yet there are new stories to be made,
little ones coming up over the horizon*

Bless the arms and hands of this land, for they remake and restore
beauty in this land

*We were held in the circle around these lands by song, and re-
minded by the knowers that not one is over the other, no human
above the bird, no bird above the insect, no wind above the grass*

Bless the heart of this land on its knees planting food beneath the
eternal circle of breathing, swimming and walking this land

*The heart is a poetry maker. There is one heart, said the poetry
maker, one body and all poems make one poem and we do not use
words to make war on this land*

Bless the gut labyrinth of this land, for it is
the center of unknowing in this land

Bless the femaleness and maleness of this land, for each holds the
fluent power of becoming in this land

*When it was decided to be in this manner here in this place, this
land, all the birds made a birdly racket from indigo sky holds*

Bless the two legs and two feet of this land, for the sacred always
walks beside the profane in this land

*These words walk the backbone of this land, massaging the tissue
around the cord of life, which is the tree of life, upon which this
land stands*

Bless the destruction of this land, for new shoots will rise up
from fire, floods, earthquakes and fierce winds to make new
this land

*We are land on turtle's back—when the weight of greed overturns
us, who will recall the upright song of this land*

Bless the creation of new land, for out of chaos we will be com-
pelled to remember to bless this land

The smallest one remembered, the most humble one, the one whose voice you'd have to lean in a thousand years to hear—we will begin there

Bless us, these lands, said the rememberer. These lands aren't our lands. These lands aren't your lands. We are this land.

And the blessing began a graceful moving through the grasses of time, from the beginning, to the circling around place of time, always moving, always

Mvto, mvto, mvto, mvto.

.

ACKNOWLEDGMENTS

Map of Trail of Tears reproduced from *Bending Their Way Onward: Creek Indian Removal in Documents* by Christopher D. Haveman by permission of the University of Nebraska Press. Cartography by Sarah Mattics and Kiersten Fish.

"Break My Heart," *The Eloquent Poem: 128 Contemporary Poems and Their Making*, edited by Elise Paschen, Persea Press, 2019.

"My grandfather Monahwee . . ." "I am going away. I have brought you this picture—I wish you to take it and hang it up in your house, that when your children look at it, you can tell them what I have been . . . for when I cross the great river, my desire is that I may never again see the face of a white man." p. 8 is from Thomas L. McKenney and John Hall, *History of the Indian Tribes of North America, with Biographical Sketches and Anecdotes of the Principal Chiefs. Embellished with One Hundred and Twenty Portraits, from the Indian Gallery in the Department of War, at Washington.* 3 vols. Philadelphia: Edward C. Biddle, 1836–44. Painted by Charles Bird King, published as prints by McKenney & Hall, 1785–1862.

"The Fight," *T. C. Cannon: At the Edge of America*, Peabody Essex Museum, 2018, p. 78.

"Directions to You" reprinted by permission of Rainy Dawn Ortiz.

"Weapons, Or What I Have Taken in My Hands to Speak When I Have No Words," *T. C. Cannon: At the Edge of America*, Peabody Essex Museum, 2018, p. 77.

"Once I looked at the moon" excerpt from N. Scott Momaday, *The Way to Rainy Mountain*, University of New Mexico Press, 1969, reprinted by permission of the University of New Mexico Press.

"The Story Wheel," *Grist: A Journal of the Literary Arts*, no. 12, 2019, p. 298.

"Washing My Mother's Body," *Grist: A Journal of the Literary Arts*, no. 12, 2019, pp. 293–97.

"Rising and Falling," *About Place* 5, no. 3, May 2019.

"Mama and Papa Have the Going Home Shiprock Blues," *T. C. Cannon: At the Edge of America*, Peabody Essex Museum, 2018, pp. 74–76. Section 8, "All the Tired Horses in the Sun" also appeared in *American Poets Magazine*.

"My great-grandfather Monahwee . . ." *Bending Their Way Onward, Creek Indian Removal in Documents*, edited and annotated by Christopher Haveman, University of Nebraska Press, 2018, p. 327

"How to Write a Poem in a Time of War," *Poetry*, September 2017, pp. 498–501.

"First Morning," *Cutthroat, a Journal of the Arts* 24, Spring 2019, p. 27.

"Singing Everything," *Cutthroat, a Journal of the Arts* 24, Spring 2019, p. 24.

"For Earth's Grandsons," *About Place* 5, no. 3, May 2019.

"Running," *The New Yorker*, July 9 & 16, 2018, pp. 40–41.

"I'm Nobody! Who Are You?" Emily Dickinson, *The Poems of Emily Dickinson*, edited by Thomas H. Johnson, Belknap Press of Harvard University Press, Copyright © 1951, 1955 by the President and Fellows of Harvard College. Copyright © renewed 1979, 1983 by the President and Fellows of Harvard College. Copyright © 1914, 1918, 1919, 1924, 1929, 1930, 1932, 1935, 1937, 1942, by Martha Dickinson Bianchi. Copyright © 1952, 1957, 1958, 1963, 1965, by Mary L. Hampson.

"Bourbon and Blues," *T. C. Cannon: At the Edge of America*, Peabody Essex Museum, 2018, p. 79. The line *"Break on through to the other side"* is based on "Break On Through" by Jim Morrison and the Doors.

"My Great-Aunt Ella Monahwee Jacobs's Testimony," Interview with my great-aunt, accessed at https://ualrexhibits.org/trailoftears/eyewitness-accounts/elsie-edwards-interview-1937/ (from the Oklahoma and Indian Territory, Indian and Pioneer Historical Collection, 1937). Public domain.

"Let There Be No More Regrets," *Bears Ears: Views from a Sacred Land*, edited by Stephen Strom and Rebecca Robinson, George F. Thompson Publishing, 2018.

"Tobacco Origin Story" (from a story of how the tobacco plant came to our people, told to me by my cousin George Coser Jr.), *Poetry*, September 2017, pp. 494–95.

"Redbird Love," *Poetry*, September 2017, pp. 496–97.

"Becoming Seventy," *Poetry*, September 2017, pp. 502–9.

"By the Way," *The New Yorker*, December 5, 2016, p. 52.

"An American Sunrise" (Golden Shovel poem from Gwendolyn Brooks's poem "We Real Cool: *The Pool Players. Seven at the Golden Shovel*"), *Poetry*, February 2017, p. 468, as part of a special selection from *The Golden Shovel Anthology: New Poems Honoring Gwendolyn Brooks* edited by Peter Kahn, Ravi Shankar, and Patricia Smith, University of Arkansas Press, 2017.

Mvto/thank you, and with much gratitude to the Guggenheim Foundation, the Academy of American Poets, the Poetry Foundation, and the Ford Foundation for assistance in poetry, song, story, and community making—

Mvto Jill Bialosky, who has helped for several years to give my poetry a place to live in the world. May all good things return to you, wrapped in poetry. And for Kathy Anderson, fierce guardian agent!

Mvto for my advisors, and first readers of parts or all of this manuscript and poems: Laura Coltelli, George Coser Jr., Dunya Mikhail, LeAnne Howe, Jennifer Kreisberg, Owen C. Sapulpa, Shangyang Fang, Jeremy Michael Reed, Jennifer Foerster, Ratonia Clayton, Elise Paschen, Rainy Ortiz, Natalie Diaz and Mary Kathryn Nagle. I have benefited from your sharp ears, eyes, and faith.

Mvto Rosemary McCombs Maxey for your assistance in translation of "Beyond" and "Welcoming Song," for your ongoing care of our Mvskoke language, and for your chicken stories.

Mvto T. C. Cannon (RIP), his sister Joyce Cannon Yi, and all the Institute of American Indian Arts (IAIA) teachers, staff, and students who walked together back then toward fresh vision in the arts. Many trails of tears met there at that school, in that time.

Those tears were used as materials for creating powerful art of many kinds of expression.

Mvto University of Tennessee, Knoxville, English Department and Creative Writing Program staff, faculty, and students who welcomed me and gave me family. You will continue to inspire me. And for the members and advisors of NASA, the Native American Student Association at UTK, who were our circle fire of Native community there.

Mvto Melissa Pritchard, Philip Schley, and Billy Winn who welcomed our return to our homelands near Columbus, Georgia. We shared history, poetry, and walked together through fields of blood memory, and along the Chattahoochee River where my husband's and my family were forcibly removed. We could hear the Old Ones, life going on as it always will.

Mvto to my family on the other side who continue to advise me: my mother, father, my grandparents especially Henry M. Harjo, Katie Monahwee, Leona May Evans Baker, Aunt Lois Harjo, Naomi Harjo, my sister/mother Sandy Aston, John Jacobs, and all those whose names I do not know, who have not lost faith and belief in me and continue to walk with me and inspire.

Mvto for my children, grandchildren, and great-grandchildren by blood and by heart. The Old Ones say they are all our children.

Mvto for my people at home. For your vnvketkv, bravery, humbleness, and your will to carry the spirit of us the terrible distance. You keep it alive, all this way, all these years.

Mvto, my heart and inspiration: Owen Chopoksa Sapulpa.

And then there was that little black dog who used to always follow Monahwee, she told me, as we watched the sun go down over supper in Okmulgee.

ABOUT THE AUTHOR

Joy Harjo is an enrolled member of the Muscogee Creek Nation and was named Poet Laureate of the United States in 2019. Her 2015 poetry collection, *Conflict Resolution for Holy Beings*, made the short list for the Griffin Poetry Prize and was named an American Library Association Notable Book of the Year. Her awards include the prestigious Ruth Lilly Poetry Prize from the Poetry Foundation, the Jackson Poetry Prize from Poets & Writers, the Wallace Stevens Award from the Academy of American Poets, and a Guggenheim Fellowship. Her memoir *Crazy Brave* won the PEN Center USA Literary Award for Creative Nonfiction. Her one-woman show *Wings of Night Sky, Wings of Morning Light* is now available in book form from Wesleyan University Press. Harjo has produced four award-winning music albums, including *Winding Through the Milky Way* for which she received a Native American Music Award for best female artist of the year. She performs extensively nationally and internationally. Harjo is a founding member of For Girls Becoming, an arts mentorship program for young women of her tribal nation. Her forthcoming work includes *When the Light of the World Was Subdued: A Norton Anthology of Indigenous Nations Poetry* and *We Were There When Jazz Was Invented*, a musical play. She is a chancellor of the Academy of American Poets and holds a Tulsa Artist Fellowship. She lives in Tulsa, Oklahoma.